Breaking Barriers: LGBTQ Rights and Social Justice

Swatantra Bahadur

Published by Swatantra Bahadur, 2023.

While every precaution has been taken in the preparation of this book, the publisher assumes no responsibility for errors or omissions, or for damages resulting from the use of the information contained herein.

BREAKING BARRIERS: LGBTQ RIGHTS AND SOCIAL JUSTICE

First edition. March 21, 2023.

Copyright © 2023 Swatantra Bahadur.

ISBN: 979-8215493090

Written by Swatantra Bahadur.

BREAKING BARRIERS: LGBTQ RIGHTS AND SOCIAL JUSTICE

SWATANTRA BAHADUR

Exploring the Fight for Equality and Inclusion in the 21st Century

I. Introduction

- Definition of LGBTQ+ community
- Importance of understanding LGBTQ+ community
- Brief history of the LGBTQ+ rights movement

II. Sexual Orientation and Gender Identity

- Definition of sexual orientation and gender identity

- Different types of sexual orientations (lesbian, gay, bisexual, pansexual, etc.)

- Different types of gender identities (transgender, non-binary, genderqueer, etc.)

- Common misconceptions and stereotypes about sexual orientation and gender identity

III. Coming Out

- What does it mean to come out?
- Why coming out is important
- Challenges of coming out
- How to be a supportive ally for someone coming out

IV. LGBTQ+ Rights

- History of LGBTQ+ rights movement
- Current state of LGBTQ+ rights
- Major legal victories for the LGBTQ+ community
- Ongoing challenges for the LGBTQ+ community

V. LGBTQ+ Community and Mental Health

- Prevalence of mental health issues in the LGBTQ+ community
- Factors that contribute to mental health issues
- How to support mental health and well-being in the LGBTQ+ community

VI. LGBTQ+ Relationships

- Types of LGBTQ+ relationships
- Challenges of LGBTQ+ relationships
- Healthy communication in LGBTQ+ relationships
- Common relationship issues and how to address them

VII. Parenting and Families

- LGBTQ+ parenting and adoption
- Family dynamics in the LGBTQ+ community
- Common challenges for LGBTQ+ families
- Resources for LGBTQ+ families

VIII. LGBTQ+ in the Workplace

- Challenges faced by LGBTQ+ individuals in the workplace
- Workplace discrimination and harassment
- Policies and laws protecting LGBTQ+ individuals in the workplace
- Strategies for creating a more inclusive workplace

IX. LGBTQ+ in Society

- Representation of LGBTQ+ individuals in media and popular culture
- LGBTQ+ movements and activism
- LGBTQ+ role models and influencers
- The future of the LGBTQ+ community

X. Conclusion

- Recap of key points
- Importance of continuing to learn about and support the LGBTQ+ community
- Final thoughts and resources for further education and support.

I. Introduction

Welcome to our lesson on "Introduction to Lesbian, gay, bisexual, and transgender community"!

In this lesson, we will learn about the LGBTQ+ community, their history, and the challenges they face. We will also discuss the different terms related to sexual orientation and gender identity.

Let's start with the definition of the LGBTQ+ community. It is a group of people who identify as lesbian, gay, bisexual, transgender, queer/questioning, intersex, asexual, and/or any other non-heterosexual or non-cisgender identity. Members of the LGBTQ+ community have historically faced discrimination, persecution, and marginalization due to their sexual orientation and gender identity.

Next, we will discuss the different terms related to sexual orientation and gender identity. Sexual orientation refers to the gender or genders that a person is attracted to. Some common sexual orientations include heterosexual, homosexual, bisexual, pansexual, and asexual.

Gender identity refers to the gender that a person identifies as, which may or may not be the same as their biological sex. Some common gender identities include male, female, transgender, non-binary, genderqueer, and intersex.

It's important to note that sexuality and gender identity exist on a spectrum, and not everyone fits neatly into one category. Some people may identify as a combination of different sexual orientations or gender identities, and their identities may also change over time.

Now, let's talk about the history of the LGBTQ+ community. Throughout history, members of the LGBTQ+ community have faced discrimination and persecution. However, the modern LGBTQ+ rights

movement began in the late 1960s with the Stonewall riots, which were a series of protests in response to police raids at a gay bar in New York City.

Since then, the LGBTQ+ rights movement has made significant progress, including the legalization of same-sex marriage in many countries and the implementation of anti-discrimination laws. However, discrimination and prejudice still exist, and many members of the LGBTQ+ community continue to face challenges in their everyday lives.

Finally, we will discuss the challenges faced by the LGBTQ+ community. These challenges include discrimination, hate crimes, bullying, and mental health issues. Members of the LGBTQ+ community also face challenges related to coming out and finding acceptance from their families, friends, and society at large.

In conclusion, the LGBTQ+ community is an important and diverse group of individuals who have historically faced discrimination and persecution. It's important to learn about the different terms related to sexual orientation and gender identity and to understand the challenges faced by members of the LGBTQ+ community. By doing so, we can create a more inclusive and accepting society for everyone.

1. Definition of LGBTQ+ community

The LGBTQ+ community is a group of people who identify as lesbian, gay, bisexual, transgender, queer/questioning, intersex, asexual, and/or any other non-heterosexual or non-cisgender identity. This community is made up of individuals who share common experiences, challenges, and histories related to their sexual orientation and/or gender identity. The acronym "LGBTQ+" is often used as an umbrella term to represent the diverse range of identities and experiences within the community.

2. Importance of understanding LGBTQ+ community

There are several reasons why it is important to understand the LGBTQ+ community:

1. Promoting Equality: Understanding the LGBTQ+ community helps promote equality and reduce discrimination. By acknowledging and respecting the rights of LGBTQ+ individuals, we can help create a more inclusive society.
2. Supporting Mental Health: Members of the LGBTQ+ community often face mental health challenges due to discrimination, prejudice, and isolation. Understanding their experiences can help us provide support and create a safe environment where they can thrive.
3. Building Positive Relationships: Building positive relationships with members of the LGBTQ+ community can broaden our perspectives and help us connect with people from different backgrounds.
4. Creating Safer Spaces: Understanding the needs of the LGBTQ+ community can help us create safer spaces, such as schools and workplaces, where they can feel accepted and valued.
5. Advocating for Change: Understanding the issues and challenges faced by the LGBTQ+ community can help us advocate for change and push for policies that promote equality and protect their rights.

Overall, understanding the LGBTQ+ community is an important step towards creating a more just and inclusive society for all individuals, regardless of their sexual orientation or gender identity.

3. Brief history of the LGBTQ+ rights movement

The LGBTQ+ rights movement is a social and political movement that advocates for the rights of lesbian, gay, bisexual, transgender, and queer/questioning individuals. The movement has its roots in the early 20th century, but it gained momentum in the 1960s and 1970s.

One of the most significant events in the history of the LGBTQ+ rights movement was the Stonewall riots in 1969. The riots were a series of protests that began in response to a police raid on the Stonewall Inn, a gay bar in New York City. The protests lasted for several days and were marked by clashes between the police and LGBTQ+ activists.

The Stonewall riots are widely seen as a turning point in the LGBTQ+ rights movement, and they inspired the creation of many LGBTQ+ rights organizations and advocacy groups. In the years that followed, the movement gained momentum, with LGBTQ+ activists pushing for legal protections and recognition of their rights.

In 1973, the American Psychiatric Association removed homosexuality from its list of mental disorders, a move that was seen as a major victory for the LGBTQ+ rights movement. In the years that followed, many countries began to decriminalize homosexuality and recognize LGBTQ+ rights, with the Netherlands becoming the first country to legalize same-sex marriage in 2001.

Today, the LGBTQ+ rights movement continues to push for greater recognition and protections for LGBTQ+ individuals, including legal recognition of non-binary gender identities, protections against discrimination in housing and employment, and access to healthcare and other essential services.

II.Sexual Orientation and Gender Identity

Sexual orientation and gender identity are two distinct but related concepts. Sexual orientation refers to an individual's emotional and sexual attraction to others. It is often classified into three categories: heterosexual, homosexual, and bisexual. However, it is important to note that sexual orientation exists on a spectrum, and not everyone fits neatly into these categories.

Gender identity, on the other hand, refers to an individual's internal sense of their own gender. This can include male, female, non-binary, genderqueer, and other identities. Gender identity is not necessarily linked to biological sex or sexual orientation. Transgender individuals are those whose gender identity does not align with the gender they were assigned at birth.

It is important to understand and respect both sexual orientation and gender identity as integral parts of a person's identity. Discrimination and prejudice against individuals based on their sexual orientation or gender identity is a form of discrimination that can have negative impacts on their mental and physical health. It is important to create inclusive environments where individuals feel safe and valued regardless of their sexual orientation or gender identity.

1. Definition of sexual orientation and gender identity

Sexual orientation refers to an individual's emotional and sexual attraction to others, such as to individuals of the same gender (homosexual), opposite gender (heterosexual), or multiple genders (bisexual or pansexual).

Gender identity refers to an individual's internal sense of their own gender, which may be different from the gender they were assigned at birth. Gender identity can be male, female, non-binary, genderqueer, or any other gender identity that is not exclusively male or female. It is important to understand and respect both sexual orientation and gender identity as integral parts of a person's identity. Discrimination and prejudice against individuals based on their sexual orientation or gender identity is a form of discrimination that can have negative impacts on their mental and physical health.

2. Different types of sexual orientations (lesbian, gay, bisexual, pansexual, etc.)

There are several different types of sexual orientations, including:

1. Heterosexual: Sexual attraction to individuals of the opposite gender.
2. Homosexual: Sexual attraction to individuals of the same gender.
3. Bisexual: Sexual attraction to individuals of both the same and opposite genders.
4. Pansexual: Sexual attraction to individuals of any gender identity, including non-binary and genderqueer individuals.
5. Asexual: A lack of sexual attraction to others.
6. Demisexual: Sexual attraction only develops after a strong emotional connection has been formed.
7. Queer: An umbrella term that can include any sexual orientation or gender identity that falls outside of heterosexual and cisgender norms.

It is important to remember that sexual orientation exists on a spectrum and not everyone fits neatly into these categories. It is also important to respect and support individuals regardless of their sexual orientation or gender identity.

3. Different types of gender identities (transgender, non-binary, genderqueer, etc.)

There are several different types of gender identities, including:

1. Cisgender: An individual whose gender identity aligns with the sex they were assigned at birth.
2. Transgender: An individual whose gender identity does not align with the sex they were assigned at birth.
3. Non-binary: An umbrella term for individuals who do not identify exclusively as male or female.
4. Genderqueer: An individual who identifies outside of the gender binary (male/female) and may identify as a combination of genders or as a gender that is not exclusively male or female.
5. Agender: An individual who does not have a gender identity.
6. Two-spirit: A term used in some Indigenous cultures to describe a person who has both a male and a female spirit.

It is important to remember that gender identity exists on a spectrum and not everyone fits neatly into these categories. It is also important to respect and support individuals regardless of their gender identity or expression.

4. Common misconceptions and stereotypes about sexual orientation and gender identity

There are many misconceptions and stereotypes about sexual orientation and gender identity. Some of the most common include:

1. Myth: Sexual orientation is a choice. Reality: Sexual orientation is not a choice and is often determined by biological, psychological, and environmental factors.
2. Myth: Transgender individuals are confused or mentally ill. Reality: Gender dysphoria, the condition of feeling discomfort or distress due to a mismatch between one's gender identity and sex assigned at birth, is recognized as a legitimate medical condition.
3. Myth: Bisexual individuals are confused or promiscuous. Reality: Bisexual individuals experience sexual and emotional attraction to both the same and opposite genders, and their attraction is valid and real.
4. Myth: Non-binary individuals are just going through a phase. Reality: Non-binary individuals have a valid and real gender identity that is outside of the traditional male/female binary.
5. Myth: LGBTQ+ individuals are more likely to be pedophiles or engage in risky sexual behavior. Reality: There is no evidence to support these harmful stereotypes. LGBTQ+ individuals are just as likely as heterosexual individuals to engage in healthy and consensual sexual behavior.

It is important to recognize and challenge these harmful misconceptions and stereotypes about sexual orientation and gender identity. They can contribute to discrimination and prejudice, which can have negative impacts on the mental and physical health of LGBTQ+ individuals.

III. Coming out

1. What does it mean to come out?

Coming out refers to the process of disclosing one's sexual orientation or gender identity to others. It can be a difficult and emotional process that involves sharing one's personal identity with others, which can be met with acceptance, rejection, or indifference.

Coming out is an individual decision and can happen at any point in a person's life. It is important to note that coming out is not a one-time event, as individuals may need to come out multiple times to different people in their lives. Additionally, not everyone chooses to come out, as it can be a complex and personal decision that is influenced by a variety of factors, such as safety concerns or cultural norms.

While coming out can be challenging, it can also be a liberating and empowering experience. It allows individuals to live more authentically and openly, and can lead to greater self-esteem and sense of belonging within the LGBTQ+ community. It is important to create a supportive and accepting environment for individuals who choose to come out, and to respect their individual journey and decision-making process.

2. Why coming out is important

Coming out is important for several reasons:

1. Authenticity: By coming out, LGBTQ+ individuals can live more authentically and openly, without hiding or denying a fundamental part of their identity.
2. Self-acceptance: Coming out can lead to greater self-acceptance and self-esteem, as individuals no longer feel the need to hide or suppress their true selves.
3. Connection: Coming out can allow individuals to connect with others in the LGBTQ+ community, providing a sense of belonging and social support.
4. Education: Coming out can also serve as an opportunity to educate others about the diversity of sexual orientations and gender identities, and to challenge stereotypes and prejudices.
5. Advocacy: By coming out, individuals can become advocates for LGBTQ+ rights and visibility, promoting greater acceptance and understanding in society.

However, it is important to recognize that coming out can also be a difficult and emotional process, and individuals should only come out when they feel safe and ready to do so. It is important to create a supportive and accepting environment for individuals who choose to come out, and to respect their individual journey and decision-making process.

3. Challenges of coming out

Coming out can be a challenging and emotional process for many LGBTQ+ individuals, and there are several common challenges that they may face:

1. Rejection: One of the biggest fears of coming out is the possibility of rejection from family, friends, and community members. LGBTQ+ individuals may worry that they will be shunned or disowned by those they care about.
2. Safety: In some cases, coming out can put individuals at risk of physical harm or discrimination, especially in cultures or communities where LGBTQ+ identities are stigmatized or even criminalized.
3. Internalized homophobia/transphobia: Even if LGBTQ+ individuals are accepting of their own identity, they may still struggle with internalized homophobia/transphobia, or negative beliefs and attitudes about themselves due to societal stigma and discrimination.
4. Emotional strain: Coming out can be a highly emotional and stressful process, especially if individuals are met with negative reactions or lack of understanding from those they come out to.
5. Constantly coming out: As previously mentioned, coming out is not a one-time event, and individuals may have to come out repeatedly to different people throughout their lives.

It is important to create a supportive and accepting environment for individuals who choose to come out, and to recognize the challenges they may face. Providing emotional support, access to resources, and promoting acceptance and understanding can help alleviate some of the challenges of coming out.

4. How to be a supportive ally for someone coming out

Being a supportive ally for someone who is coming out as LGBTQ+ involves creating a safe and accepting environment for them to share their identity and offering support throughout their journey. Here are some ways to be a supportive ally:

1. Listen: One of the most important things you can do as an ally is to listen to the LGBTQ+ individual and provide a safe space for them to express themselves.
2. Educate yourself: Educate yourself about the LGBTQ+ community and the challenges they face, so that you can better understand their experiences and be a more informed ally.
3. Show support: Show your support by using inclusive language, respecting their pronouns and name, and standing up against discrimination or prejudice.
4. Be patient: Remember that coming out can be a complex and emotional process, and that individuals may need time and support to come to terms with their identity.
5. Offer resources: Offer resources such as LGBTQ+ organizations, support groups, or counseling services that can provide additional support and resources.
6. Respect their privacy: It is important to respect the individual's privacy and not to share their identity without their permission.

By being a supportive ally, you can help create a more accepting and inclusive environment for LGBTQ+ individuals, and show your commitment to their well-being and dignity.

IV. LGBTQ+ Rights

LGBTQ+ rights refer to the legal protections and equal treatment of individuals who identify as lesbian, gay, bisexual, transgender, or queer. Despite progress in recent years, LGBTQ+ individuals still face discrimination and inequalities in many areas of society, including:

1. Employment: LGBTQ+ individuals may face discrimination in the workplace, including being denied jobs or promotions, or being harassed or fired because of their sexual orientation or gender identity.
2. Housing: LGBTQ+ individuals may face discrimination when trying to rent or buy a home, or may be denied access to housing based on their identity.
3. Healthcare: LGBTQ+ individuals may experience discrimination and lack of access to healthcare services, including necessary medical treatments related to their gender identity or sexual orientation.
4. Education: LGBTQ+ individuals may face harassment, bullying, and discrimination in schools and universities.
5. Legal recognition: In many countries, LGBTQ+ individuals do not have legal recognition or protection for their relationships, including marriage and adoption rights.
6. Violence: LGBTQ+ individuals may face higher rates of hate crimes, violence, and harassment, both in public spaces and in their own homes.

Advocacy and activism have led to significant progress in securing legal protections and equal treatment for LGBTQ+ individuals, including the legalization of same-sex marriage in many countries and the enactment of anti-discrimination laws. However, there is still work to be done to ensure that all LGBTQ+ individuals are able to live free from discrimination and enjoy equal rights and opportunities.

1. History of LGBTQ+ rights movement

The history of the LGBTQ+ rights movement dates back to the late 19th century, with the emergence of gay rights organizations in Europe and the United States. However, it wasn't until the 1960s that the modern LGBTQ+ rights movement began to gain momentum. Here are some key events and milestones in the history of the LGBTQ+ rights movement:

1. Stonewall Riots (1969): The Stonewall Riots in New York City are widely regarded as the beginning of the modern LGBTQ+ rights movement. After years of police harassment and discrimination, patrons of the Stonewall Inn, a gay bar in Greenwich Village, fought back against a police raid, sparking days of protests and riots.
2. Gay Liberation Front (GLF) formed (1969): The GLF was one of the first organizations formed in the wake of the Stonewall Riots. It was dedicated to fighting for the liberation of LGBTQ+ people and promoting gay rights.
3. First Gay Pride parade (1970): The first Gay Pride parade took place in New York City to commemorate the one-year anniversary of the Stonewall Riots. Today, LGBTQ+ Pride parades and events are held around the world in support of equal rights and visibility.
4. AIDS epidemic (1980s): The AIDS epidemic brought attention to the discrimination and marginalization faced by LGBTQ+ individuals, particularly gay and bisexual men, and spurred activism and advocacy efforts to raise awareness and secure funding for research and treatment.
5. Don't Ask, Don't Tell policy repealed (2011): The repeal of the Don't Ask, Don't Tell policy allowed LGBTQ+ individuals to serve openly in the military.
6. Marriage equality (2015): The U.S. Supreme Court ruled in favor of marriage equality, allowing same-sex couples to legally marry in all 50 states.

While significant progress has been made in securing legal protections and equal treatment for LGBTQ+ individuals, discrimination and inequalities still persist. The fight for LGBTQ+ rights and acceptance continues to this day.

2. Current state of LGBTQ+ rights

The current state of LGBTQ+ rights varies depending on the country and region. While significant progress has been made in recent years, discrimination and inequality still persist in many areas of society, including employment, healthcare, housing, and education. Here are some examples of the current state of LGBTQ+ rights:

1. Legal recognition: As of 2021, same-sex marriage is legal in 29 countries, including the United States, Canada, and much of Europe. However, in many countries, same-sex relationships are still not legally recognized, and LGBTQ+ individuals may face legal penalties or imprisonment.
2. Anti-discrimination laws: Many countries have enacted laws to protect LGBTQ+ individuals from discrimination in employment, housing, and other areas. However, discrimination still occurs in many places, particularly against transgender individuals and people of color within the LGBTQ+ community.
3. Healthcare: Some countries have made strides in providing healthcare services that are specifically tailored to the needs of LGBTQ+ individuals, such as gender-affirming hormone therapy and surgeries. However, discrimination and lack of access to healthcare services remain issues for many LGBTQ+ individuals, particularly those in low-income communities.
4. Violence: LGBTQ+ individuals continue to face high rates of violence and harassment, both in public spaces and in their own homes. Transgender individuals and people of color within the LGBTQ+ community are particularly vulnerable.
5. Political backlash: In some countries, there has been a backlash against LGBTQ+ rights, with governments enacting anti-LGBTQ+ legislation and policies, or allowing discrimination to go unchecked.

While the fight for LGBTQ+ rights and acceptance has come a long way, there is still much work to be done to ensure that all LGBTQ+ individuals are able to live free from discrimination and enjoy equal rights and opportunities.

3. Major legal victories for the LGBTQ+ community

The LGBTQ+ community has won many legal victories over the past several decades, which have helped to secure greater legal protections and rights for LGBTQ+ individuals. Here are some major legal victories for the LGBTQ+ community:

1. Lawrence v. Texas (2003): The U.S. Supreme Court struck down Texas' sodomy law, which criminalized consensual same-sex sexual activity, in a landmark decision that paved the way for greater legal protections for LGBTQ+ individuals.
2. United States v. Windsor (2013): The U.S. Supreme Court struck down the Defense of Marriage Act (DOMA), which defined marriage as between one man and one woman, and denied federal benefits to same-sex couples. The ruling paved the way for legal recognition of same-sex marriage in the United States.
3. Obergefell v. Hodges (2015): The U.S. Supreme Court ruled that same-sex couples have a constitutional right to marry, making same-sex marriage legal in all 50 U.S. states.
4. Employment Non-Discrimination Act (ENDA) (2013): In the United States, the Senate passed the Employment Non-Discrimination Act, which would have banned employment discrimination on the basis of sexual orientation or gender identity. While the bill did not become law, many states and municipalities have passed similar laws to protect LGBTQ+ individuals from employment discrimination.
5. Protection against discrimination in healthcare (2021): In the United States, the Biden administration signed an executive order protecting LGBTQ+ individuals against discrimination in healthcare, reversing a Trump-era policy that allowed healthcare providers to refuse care to LGBTQ+ individuals on religious or moral grounds.

These legal victories have helped to secure greater legal protections and rights for LGBTQ+ individuals, and have paved the way for continued progress in the fight for LGBTQ+ equality.

4. Ongoing challenges for the LGBTQ+ community

While significant progress has been made in securing legal protections and rights for the LGBTQ+ community, there are still many ongoing challenges that LGBTQ+ individuals face. Here are some examples of ongoing challenges:

1. Discrimination: LGBTQ+ individuals continue to face discrimination in many areas of society, including employment, housing, education, and healthcare. Discrimination can take many forms, from harassment and bullying to denial of services.
2. Violence: LGBTQ+ individuals face high rates of violence and harassment, both in public spaces and in their own homes. Transgender individuals and people of color within the LGBTQ+ community are particularly vulnerable.
3. Lack of legal protections: While many countries have enacted laws to protect LGBTQ+ individuals from discrimination and hate crimes, in some countries, LGBTQ+ individuals still lack legal protections.
4. Stigma and social acceptance: Stigma and discrimination can have negative effects on mental health and well-being for LGBTQ+ individuals. While societal attitudes towards LGBTQ+ individuals have become more accepting in many places, there are still many places where stigma and discrimination persist.
5. Political backlash: In some countries, there has been a backlash against LGBTQ+ rights, with governments enacting anti-LGBTQ+ legislation and policies, or allowing discrimination to go unchecked.

These ongoing challenges make it clear that there is still much work to be done to ensure that all LGBTQ+ individuals are able to live free from discrimination and enjoy equal rights and opportunities. It is important to continue advocating for LGBTQ+ rights and working towards greater acceptance and understanding of the LGBTQ+ community.

V. LGBTQ+ Community and Mental Health

The LGBTQ+ community faces unique challenges when it comes to mental health. Here are some of the factors that can impact mental health within the LGBTQ+ community:

1. Stigma and discrimination: LGBTQ+ individuals face stigma and discrimination that can lead to feelings of isolation, low self-esteem, and depression. This can be particularly damaging for young people who are still coming to terms with their sexuality or gender identity.

2. Minority stress: Minority stress refers to the chronic stress that results from being a member of a marginalized group. LGBTQ+ individuals face minority stress related to their sexual orientation or gender identity, which can lead to negative health outcomes, including anxiety, depression, and substance abuse.

3. Lack of access to healthcare: Some LGBTQ+ individuals may face barriers to accessing healthcare, including lack of insurance or fear of discrimination from healthcare providers. This can result in delayed or inadequate treatment for mental health issues.

4. Trauma: LGBTQ+ individuals may experience trauma related to discrimination, violence, or rejection from family members or loved ones.

5. Intersectionality: LGBTQ+ individuals may face additional challenges related to their race, ethnicity, religion, or other identities. This can compound the effects of stigma and discrimination and lead to additional mental health challenges.

It is important to recognize the impact of these factors on the mental health of LGBTQ+ individuals and work towards creating safe and supportive environments for them. This includes providing access to mental health resources that are inclusive and culturally competent, as well as working to reduce stigma and discrimination.

1. Prevalence of mental health issues in the LGBTQ+ community

Research indicates that LGBTQ+ individuals are more likely to experience mental health issues than their heterosexual or cisgender counterparts. Here are some examples:

1. Depression: Studies have found that LGBTQ+ individuals are two to three times more likely to experience depression than heterosexual individuals.
2. Anxiety: LGBTQ+ individuals are also at a higher risk for anxiety disorders, including social anxiety disorder and generalized anxiety disorder.
3. Substance abuse: LGBTQ+ individuals are more likely to engage in substance abuse, including alcohol and drug abuse.
4. Suicide: LGBTQ+ individuals are at a higher risk for suicidal thoughts and suicide attempts than heterosexual individuals. Transgender individuals are at particularly high risk.
5. Eating disorders: LGBTQ+ individuals, especially those who are cisgender women or non-binary, are more likely to experience eating disorders than heterosexual individuals.

It is important to note that these statistics are not due to LGBTQ+ identity itself, but rather the impact of stigma, discrimination, and other societal factors that can affect mental health. Providing access to mental health resources and working towards reducing stigma and discrimination can help to address these disparities and improve mental health outcomes for the LGBTQ+ community.

2. Factors that contribute to mental health issues

There are several factors that can contribute to mental health issues within the LGBTQ+ community, including:

1. Stigma and discrimination: LGBTQ+ individuals may face stigma and discrimination from society, which can lead to feelings of isolation, low self-esteem, and depression.
2. Minority stress: Minority stress refers to the chronic stress that results from being a member of a marginalized group. LGBTQ+ individuals face minority stress related to their sexual orientation or gender identity, which can lead to negative health outcomes, including anxiety, depression, and substance abuse.
3. Family rejection: LGBTQ+ individuals who experience rejection from family members or loved ones may be at increased risk for mental health issues, including depression and anxiety.
4. Trauma: LGBTQ+ individuals may experience trauma related to discrimination, violence, or rejection from family members or loved ones.
5. Lack of access to healthcare: Some LGBTQ+ individuals may face barriers to accessing healthcare, including lack of insurance or fear of discrimination from healthcare providers. This can result in delayed or inadequate treatment for mental health issues.
6. Social isolation: LGBTQ+ individuals may experience social isolation due to stigma and discrimination, which can lead to feelings of loneliness and depression.

It is important to address these factors in order to promote mental health and well-being within the LGBTQ+ community. This includes creating safe and inclusive spaces, providing access to mental health resources, and working to reduce stigma and discrimination.

3. How to support mental health and well-being in the LGBTQ+ community

There are several ways to support mental health and well-being within the LGBTQ+ community, including:

1. Educate yourself: Take the time to learn about the unique challenges and experiences faced by LGBTQ+ individuals. This can help you better understand the impact of stigma and discrimination on mental health.
2. Provide support: Be a supportive ally to LGBTQ+ individuals in your life. Listen to their concerns, validate their experiences, and offer assistance when needed.
3. Create safe spaces: Foster inclusive environments that are welcoming to LGBTQ+ individuals. This includes advocating for policies and practices that protect the rights of LGBTQ+ individuals, and creating safe spaces for LGBTQ+ people to gather and connect with others who share their experiences.
4. Promote mental health resources: Share information about mental health resources that are available to LGBTQ+ individuals, such as support groups, counseling services, and crisis hotlines.
5. Advocate for change: Speak out against discrimination and support policies and initiatives that promote equality and acceptance for LGBTQ+ individuals. This can include advocating for LGBTQ+ rights at the local, state, and national levels.
6. Encourage self-care: Encourage LGBTQ+ individuals to prioritize their mental health and engage in self-care practices, such as exercise, meditation, and spending time with loved ones.

By taking these steps, we can support mental health and well-being within the LGBTQ+ community and work towards creating a more inclusive and accepting society.

VI. LGBTQ+ Relationships

LGBTQ+ relationships are similar to any other romantic relationship, with the same joys, challenges, and complexities. However, there are some unique aspects to LGBTQ+ relationships that are important to understand.

First, LGBTQ+ individuals may face additional challenges in forming and maintaining relationships due to societal stigma and discrimination. This can include issues such as homophobia, transphobia, and heteronormativity. These challenges can lead to feelings of isolation, low self-esteem, and mental health issues.

Second, LGBTQ+ relationships can be impacted by legal and social barriers to equality. This includes challenges related to marriage and adoption rights, access to healthcare, and employment discrimination. These challenges can create additional stressors within LGBTQ+ relationships.

Despite these challenges, LGBTQ+ relationships can be incredibly fulfilling and supportive. Research has shown that LGBTQ+ relationships have many of the same positive qualities as heterosexual relationships, including trust, intimacy, and support.

It is important to support and celebrate LGBTQ+ relationships by promoting acceptance and understanding, advocating for equality and rights, and fostering safe and inclusive spaces for LGBTQ+ individuals to connect and build relationships.

1. Types of LGBTQ+ relationships

LGBTQ+ relationships can take many forms, just like any other romantic relationship. Here are some common types of LGBTQ+ relationships:

1. Same-sex couples: This refers to relationships between two people of the same gender. These couples may identify as gay, lesbian, or queer.
2. Bisexual/Pansexual relationships: Bisexual or pansexual individuals may be attracted to people of more than one gender, and may form relationships with people of different genders.
3. Transgender relationships: This refers to relationships where one or both partners identify as transgender. These relationships can involve unique challenges related to gender identity, such as navigating medical transitions and societal stigma.
4. Queer relationships: This term can be used to describe any relationship where one or both partners identify as queer or non-binary. This can include relationships between individuals who don't conform to traditional gender norms.
5. Polyamorous relationships: Some LGBTQ+ individuals may choose to form relationships with multiple partners, either within a closed group or in open relationships.

It's important to recognize that every LGBTQ+ relationship is unique, and there is no "right" or "wrong" way to form a relationship. What matters most is that the relationship is built on love, respect, and mutual understanding.

2. Challenges of LGBTQ+ relationships

LGBTQ+ relationships can face unique challenges due to societal stigma, discrimination, and lack of legal protections. Here are some of the challenges that LGBTQ+ individuals and couples may face in their relationships:

1. Lack of legal recognition: In many countries, same-sex marriage and adoption are still not recognized, which can create additional stress and barriers for LGBTQ+ couples who want to start a family or build a life together.
2. Discrimination and stigma: LGBTQ+ individuals may face discrimination in areas such as housing, employment, and healthcare, which can put a strain on their relationships and create additional stressors.
3. Family rejection: LGBTQ+ individuals may experience rejection or disapproval from their families when they come out, which can create additional stress and impact their relationships.
4. Internalized homophobia/transphobia: Some LGBTQ+ individuals may struggle with internalized feelings of shame, guilt, or self-hatred due to societal stigma, which can impact their ability to form and maintain healthy relationships.
5. Communication issues: Like any relationship, communication is key in LGBTQ+ relationships. However, LGBTQ+ individuals may face additional challenges in communicating about their needs, desires, and concerns due to societal stigma and fear of judgment.

Despite these challenges, many LGBTQ+ relationships are able to thrive and grow through mutual support, communication, and understanding. It's important to support and advocate for LGBTQ+ rights and equality to help create a more accepting and inclusive world for LGBTQ+ individuals and their relationships.

3. Healthy communication in LGBTQ+ relationships

Healthy communication is essential in any relationship, including LGBTQ+ relationships. Here are some tips for promoting healthy communication in LGBTQ+ relationships:

1. Create a safe space: Make sure that both partners feel comfortable and safe expressing their thoughts and feelings without fear of judgment or rejection.
2. Listen actively: Listening actively means being present in the moment and fully engaged in what your partner is saying. This means putting away distractions, such as phones, and actively listening to what your partner is saying.
3. Express feelings honestly: It's important to express your feelings honestly and openly, even if it's difficult. Bottling up emotions can lead to resentment and frustration.
4. Use "I" statements: Using "I" statements can help avoid blame or accusation and create a more collaborative and supportive conversation. For example, instead of saying "you never listen to me," say "I feel like my opinions aren't being heard."
5. Practice empathy: Empathy is the ability to understand and share the feelings of another person. Practicing empathy can help create a deeper connection between partners and promote a more supportive and loving relationship.
6. Compromise: Healthy relationships require compromise and negotiation. Both partners should be willing to make compromises and find solutions that work for both parties.

By promoting healthy communication and open dialogue, LGBTQ+ individuals can form strong, supportive relationships built on trust, respect, and understanding.

4.Common relationship issues and how to address them

Like any relationship, LGBTQ+ relationships can face a variety of issues that can put a strain on the partnership. Here are some common issues and tips for addressing them:

1. Communication: Communication is the foundation of any healthy relationship. It's important to communicate openly, honestly, and respectfully with your partner. If you're having trouble communicating effectively, consider seeing a couples therapist or relationship counselor.
2. Trust: Trust is essential in any relationship. If you or your partner have trust issues, it's important to address them head-on. This may involve working with a therapist or counselor to build trust and strengthen the relationship.
3. Conflict: Conflict is a natural part of any relationship, but it's important to handle it in a healthy way. Avoid attacking your partner, and instead focus on the issue at hand. Take time to cool down if you need to and come back to the conversation when you're both feeling calm.
4. Intimacy: Intimacy is an important part of any relationship, but it can be a source of stress for some LGBTQ+ individuals. If you or your partner are experiencing intimacy issues, consider seeing a sex therapist or couples therapist who can help you work through these issues.
5. Social isolation: Social isolation can be a common issue for LGBTQ+ couples, especially in areas where acceptance is low. It's important to find a supportive community and build a network of friends and allies who can provide support and understanding.

By addressing these issues head-on and working together, LGBTQ+ couples can build strong, supportive relationships that stand the test of time.

VII. Parenting and Families

LGBTQ+ individuals and couples can become parents in a variety of ways, including adoption, surrogacy, and assisted reproduction. Here are some key considerations for LGBTQ+ individuals and couples who are starting or expanding their families:

1. Legal considerations: It's important for LGBTQ+ individuals and couples to understand their legal rights as parents. This may involve consulting with a lawyer who specializes in LGBTQ+ family law.
2. Support: Starting a family can be a challenging and rewarding experience. It's important to find a supportive community of friends and family who can provide emotional support and guidance.
3. Healthcare: LGBTQ+ individuals and couples may face unique healthcare challenges when starting a family. It's important to work with healthcare providers who are knowledgeable about LGBTQ+ health issues.
4. Parenting roles: LGBTQ+ parents may need to negotiate unique parenting roles and responsibilities, especially if they are in a same-sex relationship. It's important to have open and honest communication about parenting roles and expectations.
5. Addressing discrimination: Unfortunately, LGBTQ+ parents and families may face discrimination from others. It's important to be prepared to address discrimination head-on and advocate for your family's rights.

By being proactive and seeking support from a variety of sources, LGBTQ+ individuals and couples can successfully navigate the process of starting or expanding their families.

1. LGBTQ+ parenting and adoption

LGBTQ+ individuals and couples have a variety of options when it comes to starting a family, including adoption. However, adoption laws and policies can vary widely by state and country, and LGBTQ+ individuals and couples may face unique challenges and barriers.

Here are some key considerations for LGBTQ+ individuals and couples who are considering adoption:

1. Legal considerations: Adoption laws and policies can vary widely by state and country, and LGBTQ+ individuals and couples may face unique legal challenges. It's important to consult with a lawyer who specializes in LGBTQ+ family law.
2. Finding an adoption agency: Not all adoption agencies are LGBTQ+-friendly, and some may even have policies that discriminate against LGBTQ+ individuals and couples. It's important to research adoption agencies thoroughly and find one that is welcoming and supportive of LGBTQ+ families.
3. Home study process: The home study process is an important part of the adoption process, but it can be invasive and stressful. LGBTQ+ individuals and couples may need to be prepared to answer questions about their sexual orientation, gender identity, and relationship status.
4. Open adoption: Open adoption is becoming more common in the United States, and it allows birth parents and adoptive parents to maintain contact after the adoption is finalized. LGBTQ+ individuals and couples who are considering adoption may want to consider open adoption as an option.
5. Support: Starting a family through adoption can be a challenging and rewarding experience. It's important to find a supportive community of friends and family who can provide emotional support and guidance.

By being proactive and seeking support from a variety of sources, LGBTQ+ individuals and couples can successfully navigate the adoption process and start a family.

2. Family dynamics in the LGBTQ+ community

Family dynamics in the LGBTQ+ community can vary widely, just like in any other community. However, there are some unique challenges and experiences that LGBTQ+ individuals and families may face.

1. Coming out: Coming out can be a difficult and emotional process for LGBTQ+ individuals, and it can have a major impact on family dynamics. Family members may need time to adjust and may have a variety of reactions, ranging from acceptance to rejection.
2. Acceptance and support: Acceptance and support from family members can have a major impact on the well-being of LGBTQ+ individuals. Families who are supportive and affirming of their LGBTQ+ members can provide a sense of belonging and reduce feelings of isolation and stigma.
3. Legal recognition: Legal recognition of same-sex relationships and families has improved in many parts of the world, but there are still many places where same-sex couples are not legally recognized. This can have important implications for issues like parenting, inheritance, and healthcare decision-making.
4. Parenting: LGBTQ+ individuals and couples can become parents through a variety of means, including adoption, surrogacy, and fostering. However, they may face unique challenges and barriers in the process, such as discrimination from adoption agencies or lack of legal recognition in some places.
5. Support networks: LGBTQ+ individuals and families can benefit from support networks and communities, both online and offline. These networks can provide a sense of community, support, and resources for navigating challenges and celebrating successes.

By recognizing the unique challenges and experiences of LGBTQ+ families, we can work to create more inclusive and supportive family dynamics for all families, regardless of sexual orientation or gender identity.

3. Common challenges for LGBTQ+ families

There are several common challenges that LGBTQ+ families may face, including:

1. Lack of legal recognition: In many parts of the world, same-sex relationships and families are not legally recognized. This can have important implications for issues like parenting, inheritance, and healthcare decision-making.
2. Discrimination and stigma: LGBTQ+ families may face discrimination and stigma from individuals, institutions, and society at large. This can affect their access to resources, healthcare, and other important services.
3. Limited access to support and resources: LGBTQ+ families may have limited access to support and resources that are tailored to their specific needs and experiences. This can make it difficult to find the help and support they need to navigate challenges and celebrate successes.
4. Lack of representation: LGBTQ+ families may also struggle with a lack of representation in media, schools, and other important cultural institutions. This can make it difficult for them to find role models and positive examples of LGBTQ+ families.
5. Internalized homophobia and transphobia: LGBTQ+ individuals and families may also struggle with internalized homophobia and transphobia, which can be the result of living in a society that is often hostile to LGBTQ+ people.

By recognizing and addressing these challenges, we can work to create more inclusive and supportive environments for LGBTQ+ families. This includes advocating for legal recognition and protections, promoting LGBTQ+ visibility and representation, and providing resources and support tailored to the needs of LGBTQ+ families.

4. Resources for LGBTQ+ families

There are several resources available for LGBTQ+ families, including:

1. LGBTQ+ family support groups: These groups provide a safe and supportive space for LGBTQ+ families to connect with each other, share experiences, and receive emotional support.
2. LGBTQ+ family-friendly healthcare providers: It's important for LGBTQ+ families to find healthcare providers who are knowledgeable about LGBTQ+ health issues and who are inclusive in their approach to care.
3. LGBTQ+ family-focused organizations: There are several organizations that focus specifically on supporting LGBTQ+ families and advocating for their rights and needs.
4. LGBTQ+ family-friendly events and activities: Many cities and communities offer LGBTQ+ family-friendly events and activities, such as pride festivals, family picnics, and youth programs.
5. LGBTQ+ family-friendly media: There are a growing number of books, movies, and TV shows that feature LGBTQ+ families and address issues relevant to them.

By connecting with these resources, LGBTQ+ families can find the support and resources they need to navigate challenges, build resilience, and thrive.

VIII.LGBTQ+ in the Workplace

The topic of LGBTQ+ rights in the workplace has gained attention in recent years. Here are some important aspects to consider:

1. Discrimination in the workplace: Despite the progress that has been made in LGBTQ+ rights, discrimination against LGBTQ+ people in the workplace still occurs. This discrimination can take many forms, including being passed over for job opportunities, being subject to harassment or a hostile work environment, and being fired or otherwise penalized because of one's sexual orientation or gender identity.

2. Legal protections: In some countries, there are legal protections in place that prohibit discrimination against LGBTQ+ people in the workplace. In the United States, for example, the Civil Rights Act of 1964 has been interpreted by the Supreme Court to include protections against discrimination based on sexual orientation and gender identity.

3. Workplace policies: Many employers have developed policies and practices to support LGBTQ+ employees and create a welcoming and inclusive workplace culture. This can include providing gender-neutral bathrooms, offering healthcare benefits that cover gender-affirming care, and creating employee resource groups for LGBTQ+ employees.

4. Intersectionality: It's important to recognize that LGBTQ+ people are not a monolithic group and that other aspects of one's identity, such as race, ethnicity, and religion, can intersect with sexual orientation and gender identity to create unique experiences and challenges.

By advocating for LGBTQ+ rights in the workplace and promoting inclusive policies and practices, we can create a more equitable and just work environment for all employees.

1. Challenges faced by LGBTQ+ individuals in the workplace

LGBTQ+ individuals face several challenges in the workplace, including:

1. Discrimination and Harassment: LGBTQ+ individuals often face discrimination and harassment in the workplace, including being subjected to offensive comments, jokes, and slurs based on their sexual orientation or gender identity. This can create a hostile work environment that negatively impacts their productivity and mental health.

2. Lack of Legal Protections: In many countries, there is no legal protection against discrimination based on sexual orientation or gender identity. This means that LGBTQ+ individuals can be fired or denied a job or promotion simply because of their sexual orientation or gender identity.

3. Lack of Diversity and Inclusion: Many workplaces are not diverse and inclusive, which can lead to LGBTQ+ individuals feeling excluded and unsupported. This can negatively impact their job satisfaction, productivity, and overall mental health.

4. Barriers to Advancement: LGBTQ+ individuals may face barriers to advancement in their careers due to discrimination and lack of support. This can limit their opportunities for career growth and advancement, leading to a significant pay gap compared to their non-LGBTQ+ counterparts.

By understanding and addressing these challenges, employers can create a more inclusive and supportive work environment for LGBTQ+ individuals. This includes developing policies and practices that support diversity and inclusion, providing training to employees and managers, and actively addressing discrimination and harassment.

2. Workplace discrimination and harassment

Workplace discrimination and harassment can have a significant impact on the mental health and well-being of LGBTQ+ individuals. Discrimination and harassment can take many forms, including:

1. Verbal Harassment: This can include derogatory remarks or slurs based on a person's sexual orientation or gender identity.
2. Physical Harassment: This can include unwanted touching, physical assault, or threats of violence.
3. Exclusion: LGBTQ+ individuals may be excluded from team activities or work-related events due to their sexual orientation or gender identity.
4. Unequal Treatment: LGBTQ+ individuals may be treated unfairly compared to their non-LGBTQ+ colleagues, including being passed over for promotions or being paid less.
5. Microaggressions: These are subtle, often unintentional behaviors or comments that can be discriminatory or hurtful to LGBTQ+ individuals.

Discrimination and harassment can create a hostile work environment that can negatively impact a person's mental health and productivity. It can lead to anxiety, depression, and even PTSD. It can also lead to physical health problems, such as chronic headaches and stomach problems.

Employers should take steps to prevent discrimination and harassment in the workplace. This includes implementing policies that prohibit discrimination and harassment, providing training to employees and managers, and creating a culture of respect and inclusivity. Employers should also have a clear and accessible process for reporting discrimination and harassment, and should take swift and appropriate action when incidents are reported.

3. Policies and laws protecting LGBTQ+ individuals in the workplace

In recent years, many policies and laws have been put in place to protect LGBTQ+ individuals in the workplace. Here are some examples:

1. Title VII of the Civil Rights Act of 1964: This law prohibits employment discrimination based on race, color, religion, sex, and national origin. In 2020, the Supreme Court ruled that Title VII's prohibition on sex discrimination also applies to discrimination based on sexual orientation and gender identity.
2. Executive Order 13672: This order, signed by President Obama in 2014, prohibits federal contractors and subcontractors from discriminating against employees or job applicants based on their sexual orientation or gender identity.
3. Employment Non-Discrimination Act (ENDA): This proposed federal law would prohibit employment discrimination based on sexual orientation or gender identity.
4. State and local laws: Many states and localities have their own laws prohibiting employment discrimination based on sexual orientation and/or gender identity.

Employers should be aware of these policies and laws and ensure that their workplace policies and practices are in compliance. They should also make sure that all employees are aware of their rights and the company's policies regarding discrimination and harassment. By creating a culture of respect and inclusivity, employers can help ensure that all employees, including LGBTQ+ individuals, feel safe and supported in the workplace.

4. Strategies for creating a more inclusive workplace

Creating a more inclusive workplace is important for ensuring that all employees, including LGBTQ+ individuals, feel valued and supported. Here are some strategies for creating a more inclusive workplace:

1. Develop and implement policies that prohibit discrimination based on sexual orientation and gender identity: Employers should have clear policies in place that prohibit discrimination based on sexual orientation and gender identity. These policies should be communicated to all employees and enforced consistently.

2. Provide diversity and inclusion training: Employers should provide training for all employees on topics related to diversity and inclusion. This training should include information on how to work effectively with LGBTQ+ colleagues and customers.

3. Offer benefits that support LGBTQ+ employees: Employers can offer benefits that support LGBTQ+ employees, such as health insurance that covers gender-affirming medical treatments and parental leave for same-sex couples.

4. Create LGBTQ+ employee resource groups: Employee resource groups (ERGs) can provide a supportive community for LGBTQ+ employees. ERGs can also help educate other employees on LGBTQ+ issues and provide input on company policies.

5. Use inclusive language: Employers should use inclusive language in all communications, including job postings, company policies, and employee communications. This includes using gender-neutral pronouns and avoiding assumptions about employees' sexual orientation and gender identity.

6. Celebrate LGBTQ+ events: Employers can celebrate LGBTQ+ events, such as Pride Month, by displaying Pride flags and sponsoring Pride-related activities.

By implementing these strategies, employers can create a more inclusive workplace and help ensure that all employees feel valued and supported.

IX. LGBTQ+ in Society

The LGBTQ+ community is an integral part of society, and its members have contributed significantly to various fields, including arts, literature, science, politics, and more. However, despite progress in recent years, many societal issues continue to affect the LGBTQ+ community.

Here are some important aspects to consider when discussing LGBTQ+ in society:

1. Visibility: Despite increased representation of LGBTQ+ individuals in media, there is still a lack of visibility and understanding of LGBTQ+ experiences in society. This lack of visibility can contribute to feelings of isolation and marginalization.
2. Discrimination: LGBTQ+ individuals continue to face discrimination in many areas, including housing, healthcare, and education. This discrimination can limit opportunities and create challenges in daily life.
3. Hate Crimes: Hate crimes targeting LGBTQ+ individuals are still a significant issue, and they can cause significant physical and psychological harm. It is essential to work towards reducing these incidents and holding perpetrators accountable for their actions.
4. Political Representation: LGBTQ+ individuals continue to be underrepresented in political positions, which can impact the creation and implementation of policies and laws affecting the community.
5. Education and Awareness: Education and awareness are crucial in creating a more inclusive society for LGBTQ+ individuals. This includes educating people on the history and experiences of the community, as well as promoting acceptance and understanding.

Overall, it is crucial to recognize and address the challenges faced by the LGBTQ+ community in society, as well as work towards creating a more inclusive and accepting environment for all individuals.

1. Representation of LGBTQ+ individuals in media and popular culture

The representation of LGBTQ+ individuals in media and popular culture has been changing and evolving over the years. In the past, the portrayal of LGBTQ+ characters in media was often negative, stereotypical, or non-existent. LGBTQ+ individuals were often portrayed as deviant or immoral, and their relationships were rarely depicted in a positive light. However, in recent years, there has been a significant increase in positive representation of LGBTQ+ individuals in media.

One of the most significant changes in recent years has been the increase in LGBTQ+ characters on television and in film. Many shows now feature LGBTQ+ characters as main characters or in prominent roles, and their relationships are often depicted in a positive and authentic way. This increase in representation has allowed LGBTQ+ individuals to see themselves reflected in media, and has helped to increase acceptance and understanding of the LGBTQ+ community.

In addition to television and film, LGBTQ+ representation has also increased in popular music, literature, and other forms of media. Many LGBTQ+ artists have gained mainstream success, and their music and writing often explores themes of LGBTQ+ identity and experiences. This increase in representation has also helped to create a more positive image of the LGBTQ+ community in the eyes of the general public.

Despite this progress, there is still work to be done to ensure that LGBTQ+ individuals are fully represented and included in media and popular culture. There is a need for more diverse representation of LGBTQ+ individuals, including representation of people of color, individuals with disabilities, and individuals from different socioeconomic backgrounds. Additionally, there is a need for more representation of LGBTQ+ individuals in positions of power and influence in the media industry. By continuing to work towards greater representation and inclusion, we can create a more accepting and understanding society for LGBTQ+ individuals.

2. LGBTQ+ movements and activism

LGBTQ+ movements and activism refer to the efforts made by the LGBTQ+ community and allies to advocate for equal rights, visibility, and acceptance. These movements and activism have played a crucial role in raising awareness and achieving significant progress in LGBTQ+ rights.

One of the earliest LGBTQ+ movements was the Stonewall Riots in 1969, which occurred in response to police raids on a gay bar in New York City. The Stonewall Riots are considered a turning point in the LGBTQ+ rights movement and sparked a wave of activism across the United States.

Since then, there have been numerous LGBTQ+ organizations and movements that have advocated for LGBTQ+ rights, including the Human Rights Campaign, GLAAD, and the National LGBTQ Task Force. These organizations have worked to promote LGBTQ+ rights in areas such as employment, housing, education, and healthcare.

There have also been several major LGBTQ+ activism efforts that have had a significant impact on society, including the fight for marriage equality and the repeal of the "Don't Ask, Don't Tell" policy in the U.S. military.

Today, LGBTQ+ activism continues to play a critical role in promoting equality and advocating for the rights of LGBTQ+ individuals. From supporting transgender rights to fighting against discrimination and violence, LGBTQ+ activism remains an essential force for progress and change in society.

3. LGBTQ+ role models and influencers

There are many LGBTQ+ role models and influencers who have made significant contributions to the community and beyond. Some of them are:

1. Harvey Milk - Harvey Milk was a politician and gay rights activist who became the first openly gay person to be elected to public office in California. He was a powerful voice for the LGBTQ+ community and fought tirelessly for their rights until his assassination in 1978.

2. Ellen DeGeneres - Ellen DeGeneres is a comedian, talk show host, and actress who came out as a lesbian in 1997. Her decision to be open about her sexuality on her TV show was groundbreaking at the time and helped to increase visibility for the LGBTQ+ community.

3. RuPaul - RuPaul is a drag queen, singer, and TV personality who has been a prominent figure in LGBTQ+ culture for decades. He has hosted the popular TV show "RuPaul's Drag Race" since 2009, which has helped to increase mainstream acceptance and understanding of drag culture.

4. Laverne Cox - Laverne Cox is an actress and transgender activist who is best known for her role in the TV show "Orange Is the New Black." She has been a vocal advocate for transgender rights and has used her platform to raise awareness about issues facing the transgender community.

5. Neil Patrick Harris - Neil Patrick Harris is an actor, comedian, and director who came out as gay in 2006. He has been a positive role model for LGBTQ+ youth and has used his celebrity status to advocate for LGBTQ+ rights.

6. Bayard Rustin - Bayard Rustin was a civil rights activist who was openly gay at a time when being gay was considered a crime. He was a key organizer of the March on Washington for Jobs and Freedom in 1963, where Martin Luther King Jr. delivered his famous "I Have a Dream" speech.

These are just a few examples of the many LGBTQ+ role models and influencers who have made a significant impact on society. Their contributions have helped to increase visibility and acceptance for the LGBTQ+ community and pave the way for future generations.

4. The future of the LGBTQ+ community

The future of the LGBTQ+ community is both hopeful and uncertain. On one hand, there have been significant advances in legal rights and social acceptance for LGBTQ+ individuals, which suggest a more inclusive future. However, there is still a long way to go in terms of full equality and dismantling systemic discrimination and prejudice.

One potential challenge for the future is the possibility of pushback against LGBTQ+ rights and acceptance. In some parts of the world, there has been a rise in conservative and nationalist movements that seek to restrict LGBTQ+ rights and roll back progress that has been made. This makes continued activism and advocacy for LGBTQ+ rights and equality all the more important.

Overall, the future of the LGBTQ+ community will depend on the continued efforts of activists, allies, and community members to promote acceptance and understanding, challenge discrimination, and fight for equal rights and protections. It is a community that has shown resilience and perseverance in the face of adversity, and there is reason to believe that this will continue in the years and decades to come.

Conclusion

In conclusion, the LGBTQ+ community is a diverse group of individuals who face unique challenges in various aspects of their lives, including mental health, relationships, parenting, and the workplace. However, the community has come a long way in terms of legal recognition and social acceptance, thanks to the efforts of activists and allies. It is crucial to understand and support the LGBTQ+ community to create a more inclusive and equitable society. We must continue to educate ourselves, challenge stereotypes and discrimination, and advocate for the rights of all individuals, regardless of their sexual orientation or gender identity. Together, we can work towards a brighter future where everyone is free to express themselves and love who they choose without fear of prejudice or discrimination.

Recap of key points

Sure, here's a recap of some of the key points covered in this lesson on the LGBTQ+ community:

- The LGBTQ+ community is a diverse group of individuals who identify as lesbian, gay, bisexual, transgender, queer/questioning, and more.

- It is important to understand and support the LGBTQ+ community to create a more inclusive and equitable society.

- The LGBTQ+ rights movement has made significant progress, but there are ongoing challenges, including discrimination and violence.

- Mental health is a significant issue for the LGBTQ+ community, with higher rates of depression, anxiety, and suicide compared to the general population.

- LGBTQ+ relationships face unique challenges, but healthy communication can help address common issues.

- LGBTQ+ individuals and families face discrimination and challenges in the workplace, but policies and laws exist to protect their rights.

- Representation of LGBTQ+ individuals in media and popular culture can have a significant impact on social acceptance and equality.

- We must continue to educate ourselves, challenge stereotypes and discrimination, and advocate for the rights of all individuals, regardless of their sexual orientation or gender identity.

These are just some of the key points covered in this lesson.

Importance of continuing to learn about and support the LGBTQ+ community

Continuing to learn about and support the LGBTQ+ community is essential for creating a more inclusive and accepting society. Some key points to keep in mind include:

• The LGBTQ+ community is diverse and encompasses a range of sexual orientations and gender identities.

• Coming out can be a challenging process, and it is important to support those who choose to do so.

• The LGBTQ+ community has faced many legal challenges and continues to fight for equal rights.

• Mental health issues are prevalent in the LGBTQ+ community, and it is important to support individuals and promote well-being.

• LGBTQ+ families face unique challenges, and resources are available to support them.

• Discrimination and harassment in the workplace are still prevalent, and it is important to advocate for policies and laws that protect LGBTQ+ individuals.

• Representation and visibility in media and popular culture are important for promoting acceptance and understanding.

• Learning about and supporting the LGBTQ+ community is an ongoing process, and it is important to continue to educate ourselves and others.

Final thoughts and resources for further education and support.

In conclusion, understanding the LGBTQ+ community is crucial to creating a more inclusive and accepting society. We have covered various topics, including the definition of LGBTQ+, the history of the LGBTQ+ rights movement, sexual orientation and gender identity, coming out, mental health, relationships, parenting, the workplace, society, and more.

It is important to challenge stereotypes and support the LGBTQ+ community in any way possible. Whether it is through education, advocacy, or support, we can all make a difference. Here are some resources for further education and support:

- The Trevor Project: A national organization providing crisis intervention and suicide prevention services to LGBTQ+ youth.

- GLAAD: A non-profit organization that works to accelerate acceptance of the LGBTQ+ community through media advocacy.

- Human Rights Campaign: America's largest civil rights organization working to achieve LGBTQ+ equality.

- PFLAG: A national organization for LGBTQ+ people, their families, and allies, providing support, education, and advocacy.

- National Center for Transgender Equality: A national social justice organization devoted to ending discrimination and violence against transgender people.

Thank you for taking the time to learn about the LGBTQ+ community. We hope this lesson has provided insight and understanding.

www.ingramcontent.com/pod-product-compliance
Lightning Source LLC
Chambersburg PA
CBHW051820130726
47987CB00003B/1342